Queen of the Flower World Paradise

Written and Illustrated by Caitlin Jay

To My Husband and Children,
my greatest treasures

Long ago The People told stories of the Flower World Paradise, the land from whence life and nourishment flowed into creation.

Here the butterflies and hummingbirds flew with the Jingle Bellbirds and Trogons. They sang with the precious flowers, shining and glittering like stones above value in the rich earth. Music flows like a flower's smell, like water, over ears and through the grass in the wind, feathers on the water. It chases the butterflies over the pond and up the flower mountain. The smell is food to give strength and life.

"One must travel the Flowery Road" said the Old Ones. "This road goes from Sun's rising to setting; watch the sunflowers' faces as they follow the sun pass along it every day".

The People longed for the Flower World as they learned to plant the corn, four sided fields filled with life. They saw the bursting corn of sustenance with the butterfly and birds between and sighed for Flower World Paradise.

In the Center of the World, The People saw their way to Heaven. Each direction meeting in the middle, with the road to happiness along the way to the sky.

And they began to make beautiful pictures with the four sided shapes reminding them of the way: a flower, a vase, a carving.

The breathing caves where the springs of life sprang forth were carved into four-sided openings.

"Through the caves", they thought, "we will reach Flower Mountain".

Life, wind, breath all came from the world beyond but first through the mouth of the Beast of Death we must pass.

And Death came creeping into their thoughts and with it darkness.

Tlacaelel (tlah-kah-EL-el), who made war and drank power, was named "Woman-Snake". He called for blood to bring the life down from the Flower World Paradise and the rivers ran with it.

But the people still sang of beauty and truth.

They sang of the God of the Near and Far, of a Singer who searched for Flowers to bring back in his tilma to the Kings and Princes of the Land to show them the Flower World Paradise.

In the Cuicapeuhcayotl, greatest of the flower songs, they told of a singer who searched and was led by the Golden Hummingbird to the holy, fragrant flowers.
With joy he gathered to bring and show but then the flowers were gone.
Bitterness and pain was left in his tilma and sorrow in his heart at the lost heaven.

Good men came and talked to them as to foolish people, but they did not know of the Flower World Paradise. The killings stopped and a peace began to push through the ground.

Then The Lady came.

A simple man, one who knew the songs and could repeat each note, was her messenger to The People. He found her at the top of the Flower Mountain, more beautiful than life and love.

Surrounded by birds and flowers, she spilled upon that deserted place where death had stalked the seeds of Paradise.

She came to all with the face of a Mestizo Girl and the cross of the Spaniards at her throat.

She breathed her desire for a church, to be mother to all The People. Juan Diego brought her words to the Bishop and promised to ask for the sign.

But death stalked again and called for Juan Diego's uncle. Fearful Juan Diego fled The Lady but she found him.
She comforted him, for he was in the crossing of her arms with all her children.

She sent him East to West along the Flower Path to gather flowers in his tilma so the Prince of the Church and the lords might behold the power of her Son, the God of the Near and Far. Up the flower mountain he went and found there, among the thorns and rocks, resplendent flowers filled with the dew of the night.

He showed the holy, fragrant flowers to the Bishop, showed him the picture The Queen had given of herself. On the tilma was her image, bloomed on the cactus fibers her sacred likeness.

Behind shone the sun, whose glory she eclipsed. Beneath her feet the moon was subjected. She was clothed with the stars of the sky and flowers scattered around her robe. And on her dress, where the God-Man slept within her, was the four petaled flower. Here at last was the entrance into life, the passage to the Flower World.

Then The People believed and came to be baptized. More than the flowers in the fields they came: walking, crawling and carried. The story was told across the mountains and plains of the place where paradise and earth had kissed, where The Queen had appeared to tell of her Son. This Son, the Great God of Truth and Life, had paid their debt of unworthiness and opened the gate of the Flower World Paradise to all.

In the heart of Mesoamerica, a rich tapestry of cultures and beliefs has woven together for millennia. Long before the arrival of Our Lady of Guadalupe, the indigenous peoples of Pan-Mesoamerica shared a profound belief in the existence of a paradise, a realm of eternal beauty and harmony known as "Flower World." This ancient belief system, rooted in the intricate cosmology of these civilizations, offered a vision of a world beyond the physical realm. It was a place where nature thrived in its purest form, where flowers bloomed eternally, and where the spirits of the departed found solace and peace. The concept of Flower World was not merely a theological notion; it was deeply intertwined with the anthropological and philosophical perspectives of these cultures. It served as a guiding principle, shaping their understanding of life, death, and the interconnectedness of all beings.

For the ancient Mesoamericans, the path to Flower World was rooted in the material world and accessible through the East-West path the Sun transversed. They believed that by honoring the Earth and its inhabitants, they would earn a place in this paradise after death. The arrival of Our Lady of Guadalupe in 1531 brought a profound transformation to this ancient belief system. Her appearance, adorned with flowers and radiating a divine light, clearly claimed the fulfillment of the indigenous people's concept of Flower World. Guadalupe's message of love, compassion, and redemption offered a path to a paradise that transcended the physical realm.

The convergence of these two powerful beliefs, the indigenous vision of Flower World and the Christian message of Guadalupe, led to a profound spiritual awakening across Mesoamerica. Millions embraced the new faith, finding in Guadalupe a bridge between their ancestral traditions and the teachings of the Catholic Church.

Thus, the story of Our Lady of Guadalupe is not only a religious event; it is a testament to the enduring power of belief and the capacity for spiritual transformation. It is a tale of two worlds converging, of ancient traditions finding new life in the embrace of a divine messenger.